Ripley Readers

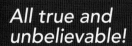

All true and unbelievable!

Learning to read. Reading to learn!

LEVEL ONE Sounding It Out Preschool–Kindergarten
For kids who know their alphabet and are starting to sound out words.

learning sight words • beginning reading • sounding out words

LEVEL TWO Reading with Help Preschool–Grade 1
For kids who know sight words and are learning to sound out new words.

expanding vocabulary • building confidence • sounding out bigger words

LEVEL THREE Independent Reading Grades 1–3
For kids who are beginning to read on their own.

introducing paragraphs • challenging vocabulary • reading for comprehension

LEVEL FOUR Chapters Grades 2–4
For confident readers who enjoy a mixture of images and story.

reading for learning • more complex content • feeding curiosity

Ripley Readers Designed to help kids build their reading skills and confidence at any level, this program offers a variety of fun, entertaining, and unbelievable topics to interest even the most reluctant readers. With stories and information that will spark their curiosity, each book will motivate them to start and keep reading.

Vice President, Licensing & Publishing Amanda Joiner
Editorial Manager Carrie Bolin

Editor Jessica Firpi
Writer Korynn Wible-Freels
Designer Rose Audette
Reprographics Bob Prohaska

Published by Ripley Publishing 2020

10 9 8 7 6 5 4 3 2 1

Copyright © 2020 Ripley Publishing

ISBN: 978-1-60991-441-7

For more information regarding permission, contact:
VP Licensing & Publishing
Ripley Entertainment Inc.
7576 Kingspointe Parkway, Suite 188
Orlando, Florida 32819

Email: publishing@ripleys.com
www.ripleys.com/books
Manufactured in China in January 2020.

First Printing

Library of Congress Control Number:
2019942264

PUBLISHER'S NOTE
While every effort has been made to verify the accuracy of the entries in this book, the Publisher cannot be held responsible for any errors contained in the work. They would be glad to receive any information from readers.

PHOTO CREDITS

Cover © Osetrik/Shutterstock.com; **3** © Osetrik/Shutterstock.com; **5** © Abramova Kseniya/Shutterstock.com; **6–7** © Philip Pilosian/Shutterstock.com; **8** © Conny Sjostrom/Shutterstock.com; **9** © Romija/Shutterstock.com; **10** © FamVeld/Shutterstock.com; **11** Mark J. Barrett/Alamy Stock Photo; **12** © Olga_i/Shutterstock.com; **14** © Edoma/Shutterstock.com; **15** © picsbyst/Shutterstock.com; **16–17** © wavebreakmedia/Shutterstock.com; **18** © Katrina Leigh/Shutterstock.com; **19** © anjajuli/Shutterstock.com; **20** © Katho Menden/Shutterstock.com; **21** © Callipso/Shutterstock.com; **22–23** © Viktoriia Bondarenko/Shutterstock.com; **24–25** © Vaclav Volrab/Shutterstock.com; **26** © Sergey Braga/Shutterstock.com; **27** © LoveEyeView/Shutterstock.com; **28** © Peter Etchells/Shutterstock.com; **30–31** © Kwadrat/Shutterstock.com; **Master Graphics** © Cattallina/Shutterstock.com, © Oleg7799/Shutterstock.com

Key: t = top, b = bottom, c = center, l = left, r = right, sp = single page, dp = double page, bkg = background

Ripley Readers

Horses

All true and unbelievable!

RIPLEY
PUBLISHING

a Jim Pattison Company

Do you know how to ride a horse?

Some horses run fast, and some can jump over hurdles!

A racehorse has a friend to help him. He is called a lead pony.

See them walking side by side?

Big draft horses work around
a farm.

Some horses have a lot of fur
so they will not get cold.

A little horse is called a pony.

Look at that funny horse
with hair on its lip!

Horses like to walk
around and eat grass.

A horse can eat from
sun up to sun down!

Do you like to eat food that is sweet? So do horses!

They will spit out food
they do not like.

You can see how old a horse is from its teeth.

The oldest horse was 62 years old!

Just like we have to clip our nails, horses have to trim their hooves!

The part under a horse's hoof is called a *frog*.

Different horses have
different names.

A baby horse is a foal.
A girl horse is a mare.
A boy horse is a stallion.

Horses come in many colors: brown, black, white, or gray.

Did you know a horse can get a sunburn?

Horses are good at seeing in the dark.

They can see better at night than we can!

A horse can sleep down on its side or up on its feet!

Do you think you could sleep standing up?

A zorse has a horse mom and a zebra dad!

See the black and white stripes on its legs?

Horses live all over the world!

Is there one that you like the best?

LEVEL TWO
Reading with help

RIPLEY Readers

All true and unbelievable!

Ready for More?

Ripley Readers feature unbelievable but true facts and stories!

LEVEL ONE
Sounding it out

LEVEL TWO
Reading with help

LEVEL THREE
Independent reading

LEVEL FOUR
Chapters

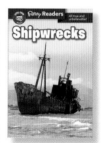

Sharks!

Trucks!

Pets

Shipwrecks

Weather

Horses

Bizarre Buildings

Dinosaurs!

**For more information about
Ripley's Believe It or Not!, go to www.ripleys.com**